THE WALL STREET JOURNAL
CARTOON PORTFOLIO

THE WALL STREET JOURNAL
CARTOON PORTFOLIO

Edited by
Charles Preston

Introduction by
Robert L. Bartley
Editor, The Wall Street Journal

DJ
DOW JONES BOOKS
PRINCETON, NEW JERSEY

Published by Dow Jones Books
P.O. Box 300, Princeton, NJ 08540

Copyright 1979 by Dow Jones & Company, Inc.

Printed and bound in the United States of America

10 9 8 7 6 5 4 3 2 1

Library of Congress Cataloging in Publication Data
Main entry under title:

The Wall Street Journal cartoon portfolio.

  1. American wit and humor, Pictorial. I. Preston, Charles,
1921-   II. Wall Street Journal.
NC1428.W33W34   741.5'973   79-20777
ISBN 0-87128-584-3
ISBN 0-87128-581-9 pbk.

This collection includes what must surely be the most deeply philosophical statement ever published on the editorial page of The Wall Street Journal. The baby bird, ready to dive from the edge of the nest, asks his mother "Any instructions, or shall I just wing it?"

What a marvelous commentary, if you stop to think about it, on the human condition. What most of us end up learning from life is that there is no substitute for winging it, that we have to learn to make our own mistakes. But at the same time most baby birds somehow do fly, and some transcendent human instincts lead us through life.

Nowhere is "winging it" more necessary than in humor. Either it's funny or it isn't. There is no instruction manual. Nothing can kill humor more quickly than trying to sort, classify and analyze it. Half the game is the surprise, the what-will-they-do-next.

The unexpected wry turn obviously fills a basic need in all of us. I think this is why our humor corner, called "Pepper . . . and Salt" has been one of the most popular and most enduring features of The Wall Street Journal. It was started in recesses of time far beyond my memory, and reader reaction continues to testify to its enduring popularity. Little wonder. With gloomy news and dark prognostications filling most columns, each of us needs a gigle now and then.

So enjoy. Here is a collection of some of the best of Pepper . . . and Salt. The bank that won't take a mantra for collateral, the metric policeman, the consciousness raising emergency.

Oh, I had forgotten. The baby bird's question is only the second most deeply philosophical statement we have published. Here is the bearded and gowned man with the plackard, "It Will Never End."

Robert L. Bartley
Editor
The Wall Street Journal

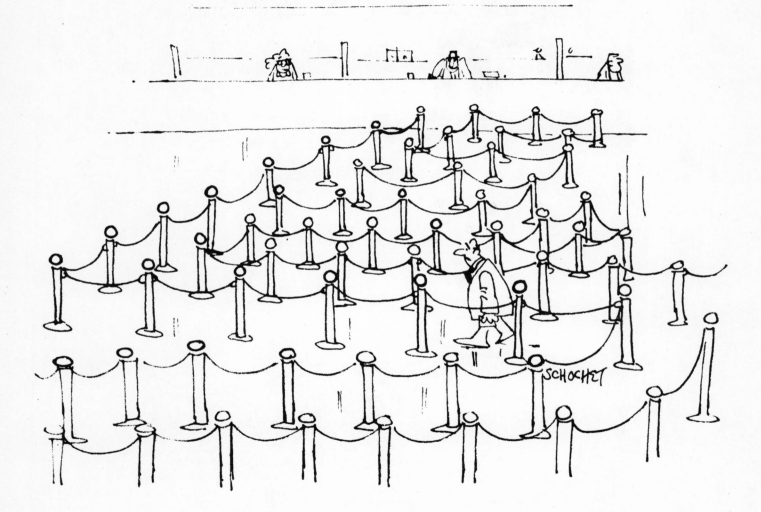

"Not only do you have water on the knee, Mr. Walters. It's polluted water."

"I've got a nagging pain right in my New York cut."

"Somehow I never thought of them as ever getting old."

"Thank you for this great honor. And I would like to take this occasion to apologize to all the boys I climbed over to make this dream come true."

"When I grow up, can I be an Arab?"

"But, Doctor, I'll be drummed out of my zero population growth chapter!"

"22 million dollars in assets and not one goddamn rubber band!"

"We're looking for some place that's totally unspoiled."

"He was a farm boy who made a fortune in the big city so he could buy a farm and become a farm boy again!"

"You've been gobbling up too many companies too fast."

"My principal objection to his lifestyle is that he's leading it here!"

"I can't say I've profited from my own mistakes. Mostly I've profited from others' mistakes."

"Does this mean the merger is off?"

"Has it ever occured to you, Leland, that maybe you're too candid?"

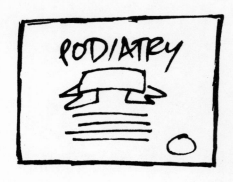

"Which toe is it that's hurting, Mrs. Turner? . . . I see — the one that had roast beef . . . ."

"That's right, Dad — I've graduated summa cum laude. What does that mean?"

"You won't get hurt if you hand over all the money, keep quiet, and validate this parking ticket . . . ."

"It was owned by a little old lady who only drove it to church on Sunday. There she goes now."

"Edwards, it's a marvelous face lift but I'm afraid retirement at sixty five is mandatory."

"I've got him softened up — now what is our product again?"

"As a firm believer in reincarnation, I'm leaving everything to me."

"I'm unwinding on company time because that's when I got wound up."

"When I was your age, I had to walk to the school bus."

"I just met the most incredible aluminum siding salesman . . . ."

"If you want me, I'll be upstairs unwinding."

"I'm sorry, Sir, but we don't sell wallpaper to gentlemen not accompanied by their wives."

"Sure it's real stone-ground wheat. Harry here was stoned when he ground it."

"Stop worrying. Politicians always promise full employment — but I've yet to see one of them deliver."

"There's a fine line between meditating and snoozing."

"I know to err is human, Hagstrom, but I'm not human."

"Federal labeling laws don't apply to homemade meat loaf."

"Hey, Dad, what war was this?"

"No more for me, thanks. My cup runneth over."

"Twenty years ago today? Of course I know what happened! The prime rate went to 6½ percent!"

"You always jump to conclusions — I did not wreck the car. It sank."

"I've found enlightenment, and I still pull down my 85,000 per. What more can I ask?"

"Mr. Holcomb, were you expecting a lynch mob?"

"He says he got that one from a goalie in Montreal."

"I'm back! Did everyone enjoy my vacation?"

"I can tell you this much — get out of transportations and
    into industrials."

UNEMPLOYMENT

"But if nobody needs a Grand Illustrious Potentate, what else will
    you consider?"

"Being of sound mind, I never worked hard enough to have anything to leave."

"Basford, I want to put an end to this rumor that you're going to be fired. You're fired!"

"Relax — — it stands for 'Island Rescue Service'."

"Thanks anyway, Helen, but Walt is spending this weekend on hold."

BURBANK

"Look Sharp, here comes the ol' man."

"Another successful year, gentlemen. We broke even on operations and pulled a net profit on accounting procedures."

"I really don't think college would be right for me, Dad. Could I just have $6,000 a year in CASH instead?"

"And let's get one more thing straight — I am not, and never have been, your 'good buddy'!"

"I've got news for you, Mr. Bloomingstone — your wife's not alone . . . I don't understand you, either."

"I'd fire Preston, if I could get his pin out!"

"Believe me, the whole economy profits. We rob someone of five grand. Then we buy some stuff from a fence. He gives his cut to the mob. They pay off the cops . . . ."

"I provided for every retirement contingency except this one."

"Is there any brand that will give my kids LESS energy?"

" 'Go ask your Mother', 'Go ask your Father'. When are we going to get some decisive management around here??"

"I can't get rid of the feeling they're going to trade me."

"I was here at Berkeley in the '60s, professor, when Berkeley was Berkeley."

"It says, 'This is your final notice. If you do not pay immediately, we will destroy your credit and have you thrown in jail. Have a happy day'."

"Yes, you did dial the wrong number. But have you asked yourself WHY?"

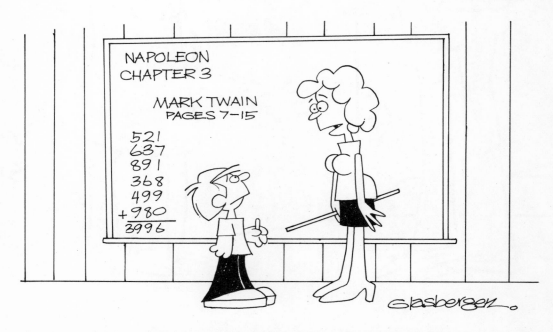

"No, Alexander Graham Bell's first words were NOT 'Can I put you on hold?'"

"Lived in this town seventy-five years. Seen a lot of changes and
    fought every damn one of them!"

"Who would have dreamed we'd be sitting here with a son at Vassar
    and a daughter at West Point!"

"None of us likes to insult their intelligence, Bolton, but it just so happens that it pays to insult their intelligence."

"Actually, I'm a little too old to believe in you, but I don't want to take any chances."

"Don't you understand, Harvey? It no longer matters about the meaning of life."

"And just how long have people accused you of being a 'take charge' type?"

"I assure you that even if I felt 'bright-eyed and bushy-tailed' I would never admit it!"

"I came up the hard way — I married the boss's son."

"Doctor, that medication you prescribed for my husband did have a side effect. He fainted when I told him what it cost."

"If not completely satisfied, return the unused portion of our product and we will return the unused portion of your money."

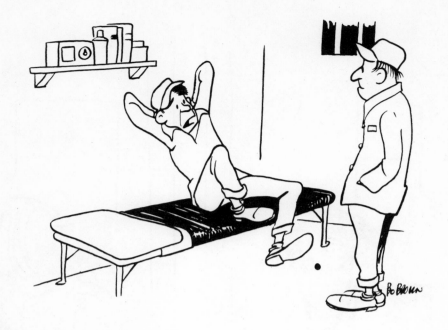

"Yessir, with what it costs the State to keep me, I could really live on the outside."

"Oh, I've found inner peace. Now I'm seeking financial peace."

"As I get it — their computer would like to talk to our computer!"

"Certainly, we're a minority group! How many multi-millionaires do you think there are?"

"Actually, we're looking for a Leo with a Scorpio ascendant."

"Polly wants some junk food!"

"This is a crime of passion. I'm madly in love with money."

"You might as well have told them my age, after bragging that we have a 5¼ percent mortgage on our house."

COCHRAN!

"It says, 'place in microwave oven for two minutes, basting every five seconds'."

"I'm afraid we can't play bridge tonight, Cynthia. Lawrence did some profit taking today and he'd like to savor it."

"Your return was neat and accurate and indicated that you understood the forms completely . . . what we want to know is how?"

"So what if we can't sell it to the kids. The adults are more gullible, anyway."

"Quit stewing about it. I'm sure they know who is what sex!"

"And if your loan payment is in the mail, please disregard these insults."

"We're going out for dinner — you've got a half hour to bathe,
change and argue about it."

"Sit anywhere. We're equal opportunity employers."

"You're a lucky man, sir . . . not many wives are interested in the mechanical aspects of an automobile."

"Go ask your mother."

"On my vacation I'm going to do things I've always wanted to do — get a haircut, shave everyday, wear a suit — —."

"Insurance forms! Government grant forms! Requisition forms! It was a lot easier being a mad-scientist in the old days!"

"It's not a war toy, madam. It's a cease fire toy."

"Hello, Consciousness Raising Institute? This is an emergency . . . ."

"I can't talk now. I'm landing a couple of fish."

"My financial plight is every bit as desperate as yours, only I haven't let myself go to seed."

"Do I have to go thru all the legal hassle for a divorce if I was married in an Electric Acid Flower Church?"

"Sure it's unfair to the little guy . . . He's the easiest one to be unfair with."

"A masters degree from M.I.T., a Ph.D. from Cal Tech, and my greatest achievement has been inventing a low-cholesterol cat food!"

"Before I was liberated, it was housemaid's knee. Now I have tennis elbow."

"It's a very rare vintage. The rest of the bottles he made that day exploded."

"Do you have a resume?"

"Everyone to the tax shelter."

"Remember the good old days when problems had solutions?"

"Why don't you look at it this way, Mrs. Peters — prices are lower today than they ever will be."

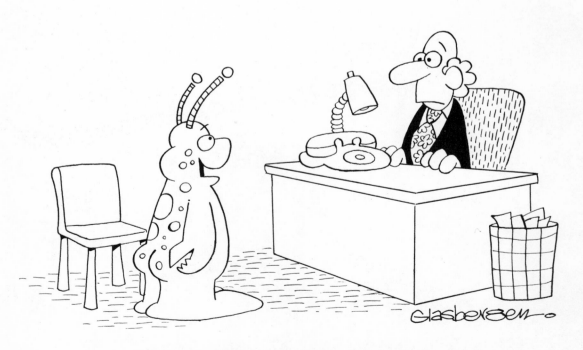

"Are you an equal opportunity employer?"

"One day I decided I was sick of doing that 9 to 5 routine — now I'm doing 6 to 10."

"May I have my allowance in Deutsche Marks, Dad?"

"You can't fire me! I owe money to everyone in this office!"

"Just answer this memo from the desk of Arthur Pring, 'Dear Desk of
    Arthur Pring' . . . ."

"Don't worry, we'll have you on your feet and out of here in no time.
    Your hospital insurance doesn't cover much."

"I'm supposed to wind it 'clockwise.' What's 'clockwise'?"

"I'm afraid we don't yet have a scientific name for the fear of high prices."

"First, the good news — You're in the running for our Chutzpah-of-the-month award."

"Hello, Johnson & Waldo, Attorneys? . . . can you sue an accupuncturist for malpractice?"

"Sorry, but a mantra isn't sufficient collateral."

"I'm sluggish — you're sluggish. Why shouldn't the economy be sluggish?"

"Joey, do you suppose there's life on other blocks?"

"The bank gives a free toaster for opening a new checking account,
but Fred gave me this fur cape for not opening one."

"Of course, money can't buy happiness, that's inflation for you."

"What kind of marriage did you have in mind? Open marriage?
Conventional marriage? Trial marriage?"

"Now they say we can't dump our industrial wastes in the river
anymore! My God! What's a river for?!?"

"Let's see now . . . was that the 28 cities in 21 days for 24 payments, or the 21 cities in 14 days for 18 payments, or was it the 14 cities in 18 days for 12 payments . . . ."

"All right, read it back to me."

"Dear Sir. Make that, Dear Wyatt. Dear Mr. Wyatt. Heh, Heh, Heh. How about letting us know . . . why don't you tell us, that is . . . uh . . . start with, we are anxiously waiting, patiently waiting . . . um . . . ."

"Who do we know with big brown eyes?"

"If there's anything to evolution, thousands of years from now people will all have bent toes."

"You say you made all these charitable deductions directly to God?"

"I don't get turned on by power any more."

"This has been a test . . . had this been an actual emergency, you can bet your booty I wouldn't still be here talking into this microphone."

"Ms. Ryan, send me in a scapegoat."

"Is there a non-smoking, non-movie and non-kiddie section?"

"There goes the neighborhood!"

"My ultimate goal? Retirement."

"This spectacle was made possible by grants from the Favius Claudius Foundation, the . . . ."

"...to my nephew, Phelps Putney, who always sneered at my conservative stuffed shirt stance, I leave him my shirts."

"Can you write me a fast, off-beat, 10-second routine for my telephone answering machine?"

"Mr. Jones, it isn't necessary for us to meet all of your dependents for your tax audit!"

"You were doing 25 millimeters in a 58 kilometer zone — er — I mean 9 meters in a 2.85 gram zone — no — that's not it — oh, the heck with it!"

ELI
STEIN

"You need a good rest — can you just wheel without dealing for a while?"

"Mr. Gorman is here to see you, sir, and I think he wants to go for your jugular vein."

"My name's BIG JOHN and I was brutalized in my formative years by a tyrannical father with whom I was forced to compete for the affection of my abusive, hostile mother . . . ."

"In all our 23 years of marriage , Albert, what do you consider the outstanding newspaper headline?"

"Open your trap."

"It's understandable. He was never happy here."

"Complicated looking thing, isn't it?"

"We've made a decision, five to one. You look stupid in that mustache!"

"I know how proud of it you are, Hodgekiss, but—"

"I would really love to grapple with this problem, but we must postpone it right now because I'm halfway out the door to catch a plane . . . ."

"Dear, is it all right if I seize power?"

COCHRAN!

"You said not to discuss religion or politics — that left only sex!"

"In the old days the air was clean and sex was dirty."

"Spell out 'miscellaneous?' M . . I . . S . . C . . E . . L . . L . . . ."

"It's your husband on two. He has a list of groceries he wants you to pick up on the way home."

"I suppose you're going to let this disco craze sweep right by you?"

"We never do anything kooky anymore."

"Some day, son, you'll probably try to take this all away from me."

"Say, Dad, can we play in your tax shelter?"

"I'm afraid medical science has no cure for negative vibes."

"What distribution do you want on this suicide note, Mr. Hinckel?"

"A place where there's a favorable rate of exchange for the Dollar? Well, there's Coney Island . . . ."

"I'm J. Calhoun Langdon who achieved, at the age of 37, the presidency of Alpha Plastics; 12 directorships; multi-multi millionaire; and one day it hit me to discover what it was all about. Now, I want to pursue this meaning and become one of the best goddam gurus in the business."

"You're absolutely sure he doesn't bite?"

"One pressure group wants us to withdraw sponsorship of our TV show,
another pressure group wants us to continue sponsorship of
our TV show, and still another pressure group wants us to add
more noodles."

"I breathe, too, you know!"

"There must be a limit to permissiveness."

"Yes, Mrs. Cargill, I know what he needs, but medical ethics prohibits me from giving it to him."

"He has reverence for all life except me."

"Whattya mean, do I have a different style? They're the first shoes ever invented."

"Cheap money or no cheap money, it's still something to be a billionnaire."

"On the other hand, what's it worth to you if I don't operate?"

"First it's Christianity, now it's the metric system!"

"Sodium Nitrite, Potassium Nitrate, Glycerin . . . ?" What is this — a pie or a bomb?"

"Now I'll turn you over to Mr. Benson who will do his best to get rid of you."

"Getting back to those interest rates, could you be a little more specific than 'it's going to cost a pretty penny'?"

"Howard, come quick — they've interrupted a commercial!"

"Any instructions, or do I just wing it?"

"Harkness, I never want to hear from any employee of mine, 'it's not whether you win or lose, it's how you play the game'!"

"Too late. Someone has already picked out all the almonds and filberts!"

"Not that kind of a leak. A LEAK leak!"

"Who says I can't argue with a computer?"

"No, dear, that wasn't one of those new high-fiber cereals. You just ate a bowl of steel wool."

"I want some no-double-fault insurance."

"No, I'm not seeking political office — I just happen to be good natured."

"Be reasonable, Mr. Lawson. You can hardly expect me to discuss the riddle of existence during the Happy Hour."

"My, what a glorious day for a proxy fight!"

"Oh, Helen — I saw the counselor today, and he told me to start paying more attention to you."

COCHRAN!

"Can't you sing anything besides, 'When the red, red robin comes bob, bob, bobbin' along'?"

PARK NOT LEST YE BE TOWED

JONIK

"Tax havens? Certainly. Do you plan to go, or will you just be sending your money?"

"We find it difficult to meet payment on our one big loan, so we'd like to change back to lots of little bills."

"Does mothers' milk still have the approval of the Food and Drug Administration?"